Sweet Soul

Distinee Gayle

Sunflower Soul

Copyright © 2018 by Distinee Gayle

For information contact:
www.fullybloomed.net

Book cover design by Divya Gurung
ISBN: **978-0-692-12097-2**

Contents

Chapter One

SEED

starting from a small, insignificant seed and transforming into the cream of the crop takes time. it takes time to grow strong roots, break through soil, keep petals intact and fully bloom.

the process is a long one but well worth the journey.

do not believe what people say,
for you are not the weeds in a garden that need to be destroyed,

you are the sunlight that keeps the flowers blooming...

~ vital

two seeds,
planted in the same soil,
exposed to the same environment,
all of the same conditions, identical...
yet we sprouted in different directions.
myself, i aimed towards the sun,
but you lagged behind in the dirt,
our roots remained connected,
but our souls never further apart.

~ growing pains

you must find strength to keep going in your weakest moments, you must find courage when you are afraid the most and you must seek sunlight in the darkest times.

you must remember that resilience is obtained through fragility, heroism is earned through fear and the sun always shines after a long moonless night.

it's essential to stay on your own path
and not stray to roads that go down any other.
follow your light and it will lead you
to exactly what you've been searching for.

sometimes i want to emerge,
like a flower blooming
on the first day of spring,
but then i remember
it is only winter
and i must be patient.

you taught me a lesson,
without even knowing.
you showed me there was
someone worth loving,
and deserving of everything
that life has to offer.

you taught me that person was myself.
from the moment i made that discovery,
life truly has not been the same.

protect your energy,
clutch it in your hands
like a pearl necklace passed down
from generation to generation
and know that it is worth more
than you could ever put
a price tag on.

little seedling,
so small and helpless,
needing water and sunlight to thrive.

little seedling,
hopeful of the beautiful plant she's going to become.
not sure if she will blossom into a cactus or a rose but knowing
that either way, she will have thorns.

over watering can cause just as much damage as under watering. one must find their balance when it comes to true needs and foolish desires.

~ aqua equilibrium

yield me from distractions.
allow me to focus,
and not let frustration
discourage me from the
greatness that is within.

growth requires patience, love and failure.
you must be willing to tolerate delay to respect time.
you must be hurt in order to appreciate joy and you must know
that being victorious in *every* battle has no value.

losing yourself is a part of the journey because you'll always end
up right where you're supposed to be – even if that was not the
destination. wandering is often far more worthy than a direct
expedition.

you sheltered me
from the summer's heat
and covered me when
winter was too cold.
no matter the season
or time of year
you were always there
to protect me.

feel freedom
flow through your body
like the wind
blowing in your hair
and have full conviction in your voice
when you tell the world
that you are liberated.
it is only in that moment
that you are released from
all of the boundaries
and borders
that you've been trapped in
all these years.

~ sovereignty

it's okay to have insecurities.
every single flaw,
blemish,
and imperfection
makes you who you are.
to own it is empowering.

the preparation leading up to being who i am
has been the best part.
growing, learning, laughing.
i'm grateful for the tears.
my failures were a blessing.
i thank the heavens for every single bad day,
because without those
i wouldn't appreciate the good ones.

surrounded by dirt, not knowing if there is even light worth
sprouting for...

it can be difficult to know whether to blossom or remain buried.

i always knew you were proud of my accomplishments,
but hearing the words come out of your mouth
was like nothing i've experienced before.
the words covered me like a blanket,
and i've never felt warmer.

~ affirmation

walking down a path
searching for happiness
isn't possible without
experiencing the obstacles
that come with the journey.
you mustn't dodge or avoid them,
but embrace every
single last one.

she grew alone,
effortlessly,
without help from
any of earth's elements
and felt proud
knowing she could do it
all on her own.

~ independence

i used to believe
my life was ending soon
when in reality
it was only beginning.

~ rebirth

i yearn to learn,
i crave to create,
and every day i desire
to be a better version of myself.

imagine being the smallest flower in the garden
surrounded by so many others
that have sprouted much higher than you...
how does one find motivation in
the mist of jealousy?

as you grow,
there are things that you must do:

bring light to areas that are dark,
let go of weight that is holding you down,
promote happiness in times of dismay,
forgive those who may not deserve it
and always remember that pain is a temporary feeling.

~ a letter to my younger self

trying to heal the wounds
that have been existing for years
is not possible.
the wounds are scars now
and time has made them mend themselves.

believe in yourself
and know you are capable
of great things.
you can often be
your biggest enemy
if you doubt your own abilities.

i feel inspired by the sky
and captivated by its colors.
every time i look up,
i become stuck in a trance
of wonder and beauty.
it's moments like this
that i feel lucky to
be alive and
able to simply admire.

i may be small now,
but give me time.
i'm setting my intentions
from this moment
that i will grow tall,
larger than life.

all i need is time.

i've wished for you to find your oasis,
in the middle of the desert...
to stumble across your haven-
a paradise created only for you,
because you deserve refuge and warmth
in this cold world, too.
i just hope that you don't have to
search hard for your nirvana
but that instead,
it comes looking for you.

you can provide love,
encouragement,
and all the water there is to offer...
but a seed will only sprout
if it desires to be close to the sun.

Chapter Two

ROOTS

i'm beginning to see what it takes to grow roots even when you're surrounded by soil. what i see as dirt, muck and grime as my domain is simply what is needed to grow my strong roots. these roots dig into the soil in which i am planted so deeply into.

i was meant to grow here for a purpose – to manifest into something beautiful.

feet planted on the ground,
firm on the land that bounds us to the earth.
the grass, the dirt. the trees, the breeze. the birds, the bees.
a connection.
the lakes and seas - so beautiful but it all comes down to me.
with my eyes open wide i can see all of life... but when i close
my lids, my mind spirals down, and my heart takes a pound.
i see no life no more.
my soul wants to be pure - i try to unlock the door.
the keys are my eyes, i open them wide.
the darkness subsides, but will the sunshine last for a lifetime?

draw yourself closer to me.
allow your mind to feed off the waves of mine,
and your heart to beat to the rhythm that's inside my chest.

i want to feel connected.
on a higher level.

~ in sync

the highest up are usually the most envied.

they are closest to the sky and for that reason are begrudged amongst others. what others don't see is that being closest to the sky means closer to the sun, making it easier to get burned.

there was a pause in our story,
a gap in time where we stopped loving each other.
we didn't know how to resume,
so we took the time to *learn* one another...
and the love came back,
like it never even left.

~ interlude

they want you to believe you aren't beautiful.
they don't want the sun to shine on you to flourish.
the environment you grow in is not loving and does not nourish
your roots.

escaping is not an option as you are planted here.
you must find ways to sprout, despite your surroundings.

i'm not saying
i wanted to push you away,
but i cannot say i regret it.
i wouldn't hesitate
to do it once more
if it meant protection over my heart.

i wanted to see the good in you,
even when it wasn't there.
i wanted to love you,
even when you wouldn't allow me to.
i wanted to change you,
but you remained the same...

sometimes we receive love that we don't deserve
and other times we don't get affection that is due to us
but we must stay true to ourselves
and know that it is a privilege to spread love
because not everyone knows how.

growing up
envious of your beauty,
i strived to be just like you.
your eyes were like diamonds
and your skin glimmered in the sunlight.

i looked at you as a perfect being that could do no wrong,
so when your diamond eyes lost their shimmer and your skin
began to lack its glisten, i started to worry.

i worried what happened to my role model and what would
happen to me for wanting to embody such a person...

had the world turned you cold or were you always this frigid?

i never wanted to become who you are now,
but who you were back then was all i ever desired.

~ artificial white roses

my ears bled
hearing all of your lies
to the point where
i tuned out anyone else speaking
just so i didn't risk feeling the pain again.

what is the reason for my lack of growth?

is there anything i could have done to make my branches grow
wider or my leaves brighter?

am i merely a product of my environment or am i at fault for my
own stagnancy?

the solution unbeknownst to me, hopelessness and despair
slowly makes its way from my roots straight to the highest point
of my being and i feel defeated.

i'm not perfect
and never claimed to be.
although you've always seen me
as flawless,
it was you who failed
to see my shortcomings.
i appreciate you for believing in me,
but wish you could see the person
inside the mold
that you've always thought
to be so enchanting.

i never understood my worth,
and i can't say that i do now...
but i do see the value
in discovering what it might be
and i think that should count for something.

i've been called conceited before,
but i've recognized my flaws,
and grew from my mistakes.
i may have walked with my head held high at times,
not to have my nose in the air
but to keep the tears from falling.

~ masque

i desire to be more kind...
to myself and others.
i desire to water my own roots more often as well as those
surrounding me struggling to thrive.
i desire to bask in the sunlight, instead of looking for shade and
encouraging others to soak in its energy as well.

i desire to not only grow, but to flourish.

imagine the moon melting into the sea
watching the horizon as the two slowly become one
waves colliding with every single crater,
washing away imperfections on the surface.

am i wrong
for loving you
through your manic
and damaging ways...
i too,
became frustrated
wondering how to mend and restore
your faith
in the power of love.
many nights
i held you in my arms
so tightly
and refused to let you go.
i just knew i could heal you
if i showed you what love was
because you'd never felt it before.

you were beautiful and bright,
but you were also loud
and explosive
just like a firework
that could like up an entire sky.

i want to leave but
i feel like i would die without you.
you've always been a huge part of me...
a part that i don't want to let go of,
but i know it's for the best...
so i've decided to break the chains
of our connection
because even if i die without you,
at least i'll be free.

hold your spirit in the palm of your hands
and lift it up to the sky.
soak in its glory, radiating from the sun.
remind yourself that although you may not see its power,
its strength is surely there.

~ ultraviolet

you hurt me in ways i never realized.

through time
your presence
became occasional
and the sharp pains in my heart
became more frequent...

but it was daily that i continued to yearn for your love.
your actions, virulent...
through time,
i learned the remedy to your poison...

and have felt empowered ever since.

~ deoxy ribon ucleic

they tell me to forget my pain,
to bury my sadness and move on...
but the real reason
that i hold on to the past
is because it's all that i have.

i walked miles through a buttercup field just to find the right one
for you.

they were all yellow and bright... begging to be picked but none
were right. i wanted nothing but the best for you because you
were the best for me.

i reached below my feet and plucked what seemed to be the
100th flower from its roots.

analyzing every centimeter from its stem to petals, i noticed a
flaw. yet again, searching for the right one i stopped and
realized.... i loved you for your imperfections. all of these flowers
were a reflection of who you are and all i could do was sit back
and admire them all.

success is often measured,
by what you have...
but in my eyes,
it is the contrary.
lack of possessions
exemplifies willingness to sacrifice
material items
for things intangible...
and that is how i define true prosperity.

it's funny how time
can show someone's true intentions,
or keep them hidden in secrecy.
it's a gamble we take
every time we play
the game of love.

~ rolling dice

the fact that the people
in my dreams
are real individuals
who i have passed
in the grocery store,
on the subway,
or in an elevator
and somehow,
someway,
remained embedded in my mind,
makes me feel connected to them...
i wonder what they were going through
the day i happened to glance their way.

have i proven to be worthy?
what will it take
to convince you
that i deserve to be valued?
there is no question
that i'd give up all of my limbs
just to feel yours wrap around me.

she was well spoken
and carried herself with poise.
when she laughed
the entire room felt her magic.
you would have never known
by looking at her
that her sparkle inside
was fading.

~ spellbound

i wish i was already who i wanted to be,
and didn't have to be molded through pain to become it.
i wish there weren't trials and tribulations,
testing my patience and endurance.
i wish i didn't have battle scars
to prove that i've been through war
but look, they're here...
they tell my story without me even saying a word.

the moon looks so divine tonight.
i close my eyes,
but can still feel its vibrancy
as it glows down onto me from the sky
and gives me permission
to fall asleep in its presence.

your skin glowed
brighter than the
marigolds in my garden
and i constantly wished
that i too,
could beam with such
golden warmth.

i was a place you came to for peace.
religiously, you were with me.
you praised my being and
whispered your hopes
and aspirations into my ears like a prayer.
you told me your fears
and asked for guidance.

the truth is, that i never had the solutions to your worries.
i let you speak, and as the words flowed out of your mouth,
so did the answers.

you spent time
praying to a false image of perfection
when it was you who ended up being the most powerful of all.

~ stained glass windows

choosing to
not give all of myself
to you is not selfish,
it is self-worth.

the sun was my source of light,
energy and love.
you blocked it from me every chance you had,
and i never understood why...
it could have been that you didn't want to see me grow,
so you hindered me from its rays...
or maybe you wanted to absorb the power for yourself.

~ eclipse

there were days where i wanted to breathe,
but my own two hands were wrapped around my neck...
and there were nights where i wanted nothing but to dream,
but my mind could only fabricate never ending nightmares.

am i at fault for my own dismay and misfortune?
or is there a higher being much greater than me,
pulling the strings on the story of my own life...

free yourself from society's standards.
break the mold they've set you in
and separate yourself from the rest.

submerge yourself in every single imperfection
as everyone else is imprisoned,
secretly admiring the features of their oppressor.

~ liberation

the love that comes to you
when you aren't even looking
is often the purest,
because it is unexpected.

you always came to me with your wretchedness,
and cried out all of your worries to my listening ear.

you told me stories of your distress,
in hopes of finding someone who could simply understand...
but instead you unknowingly passed it onto me.

your sorrow, despair
and misery became mine.
i held it with me and
every time you spoke of your torment,
my heart felt a bit heavier
and i became weak from carrying it all.

you came to me because you thought i was strong
but with time i became frail, too.

it takes billions of stars
to light up the sky.
each one small... but powerful.
important, yet insignificant in many ways.
at times, i feel like one of those stars,
lost in the sea of the sky amongst so many others.
if a single one dies and stops shining,
the others continue to do so without it.
it isn't missed or needed, despite its strength.
the sky is still illuminated and the night continues on.

i stayed close,
because i admired you.
all i wanted was to feel your energy,
but instead you drained me of mine.

it took me time to realize that
energy is transferable.
what you give into the world,
is what you get back.
one cannot expect to throw stones...
and receive diamonds in return.

Chapter Three

BREAKING SOIL

roses rise,

little flower buds bloom,

daisies bask in the light of the sun.

roses don't worry about their thorns,

the adolescent buds don't fret about possibly not blooming and

the daisies aren't the least concerned about withering in the

scorching heat.

they all just blossom where they have been planted.

they prosper and grow from each of their tiny seeds, breaking

through soil into the illuminating light of the world we call life.

if i stare into the sunrise... will the light blind my eyes or open them to new horizons?

~ perception

it scares me how one day i won't have you and you won't have
me.
our bodies 6 feet under and our souls 6 million feet in the sky.
i'm afraid that our bodies will be reincarnated into someone
new.
you won't know me and i won't know you.
i fear our paths will cross as strangers, not even knowing we had
a past.
i dread the feeling of emptiness as i walk past you, into a world
without you.

i wanted to feel special,
so i pretended
that i was the only one.
i disregarded you being distant,
overlooked the fact that
you outgrew what used to be
and ignored the way you stopped loving me.

so now,
instead of feeling special,
i feel broken and ordinary
like an old, cracked porcelain doll
sitting on a shelf
collecting dust
and not worth a thing.

~ collector's item

time seems to slip away
at times when i need it the most.
if i could hold it in my hands,
it would run through my fingers
like tiny grains of sand.

breathing in all of life's air just to blow it all out on a dream
seems silly but when it's your last breath,
it can truly be worth it.

~ dandelion wishes

i can't be the only one
who's been hurt by you
and i can tell,
you've been hurt too,
by someone once before.
they embedded their pain into you,
and you passed it onto me.
i've held onto it for quite some time now,
but i'm ready to let it go...
not by giving it to another,
but by forgiving you,
and i hope the other hearts you broke
realize it's not your fault nor their own.
i hope they find their peace
and break the cycle of desolation and destruction.

~ my wish for humanity

i try to conquer all of my battles,
and fight off all of my demons,
while trying to maintain my lucidity,
but i am scared.

i've realized,
i can still be afraid...
even though i am fearless.

i've wanted a perfect life so bad
that i was willing to sacrifice
the way i was living now
in hopes of a promising future.
my idea of perfection
slowly began to shatter
as i realized
it could never truly exist.

eloquence in young black women
is often regarded as a rarity.
diamonds are considered rare as well
but far more valued.

i've thought before
how small situations
can really change the entire trajectory
of your whole life.
i've become saddened at the thought
that if "maybe i didn't go here"
then "maybe this wouldn't have happened"
or "maybe if i didn't say this"
then "maybe i wouldn't have experienced that"
but i've also realized
that the story of your life
has been mapped out far before
your physical being ended up on earth.
there's no way to avoid these occurrences
so, there's no point in even trying.

just live.

it's easy to bury your head in the sand and not make yourself
aware of your surroundings,

but to stand on the shore and watch the waves crash, knowing
you have no control over it... is a powerful feeling.

~ consciousness

i see others with smiles,
and i am resentful of it.
i want what they have.
the radiance they have painted on their faces,
is something i've never gotten to wear.
i truly wonder what it's like to feel happy inside,
but a part of me says that they do, too.

~ semblance

they told me i was a wildfire.
they were right.
i wanted to burn everything.

he told me i was a blazing spirit.
he was right.
i wanted to light his world up.

i knew i was an inferno,
large and dangerously out of control.

~ amber

what happens when time doesn't heal all wounds
and years have gone by but i am still aching from the pain...

what happens when i simply don't have any more time left?

i do not adhere
to the laws of man
that have been created
so arbitrarily
especially
when i'm already a prisoner
of my own mind.

finding peace is a journey
that could take years to complete.
the most victorious feeling is when you realize
it was inside of you all along.

~ olive branch

sometimes i dream about leaving earth. leaving everything behind and floating into space. just imagining this makes my heart beat slower and i can hear every breath i take. closing my eyes makes no difference except for the stars that i no longer see. it's all dark but reaching my arms out, i can touch them and the tip of my fingers tingle... this is the euphoria i always imagined.

~ zero gravity

sometimes i feel unbreakable;
strong and empowered.
other days i am a fragile piece of glass;
where anything can shatter my being...
but everyday i feel something...
and feeling anything at all
is what matters most.

your coy smile,
calm behavior
and those hypnotizing eyes
had me believing
that i was the fortunate one.
i used to blush at the thought of
that same smile
but as luck had it
it was all a facade,
an illusion, and an act
that all became more transparent
as time went on.

rainbows happen when
sunlight and rain come together,
and i think that just proves
that no matter what things may combine,
something beautiful
will always appear...
even after a storm.

i used to fear getting hurt,
but now i see it as an opportunity
to show myself
how strong i really am
and how well i manage
overcoming anything
that comes in my way
or against me.

~ vigor

i wish i weren't so angry.
and that i had peaceful thoughts.
i wish i had patience,
and evil words didn't spew out of my mouth.
i wish the love inside my heart showed on the outside
and i never caused you a single moment of pain.

deception of reality
only distorts your own eyes,
rarely affecting those around you...
trapped in your own mind of despair,
pretending that hopelessness is flooding in
when you withhold the power to cease it all.

none of this is concrete
and you must learn to let go of things that are not there.

~ simulation

of all the flowers in the garden,
i used to feel like it only rained on me.
i cursed the sky every day and every night that it happened.

it took years for me to realize that every drop that fell from
above was needed in order for me to grow.

it's incredible how many of us do not welcome changes in life
but find solace and comfort from a caterpillar transforming into
a butterfly.

~ embracing chrysalis

i used to feel like i had to strip myself,
of everything on the exterior...
just so that you could see what was within.

clawing at my skin,
scraping it away,
to show you my flesh.

it is only now that i've realized
how much i took away from myself
just to give you,
and you never truly valued it at all.

i'm tired of
exposing and unfolding myself
to those who seek not to understand me
but only to define me.

my story
is not yours to tell
and i do not belong in
any of the tiny boxes
you try to fit me in.

you will never receive praise
from those who believe their way
is righteous.
they would condemn you a hundred times
before they commend you just once.

~ judgement day

i crave to know what it's like
to truly be free.
not only in body
but in mind and spirit as well...
to float into
a spiritual awakening
and leave every chain behind
that's been holding me back
on this earth
for all of eternity.

as the leaves begin to change colors,
so does the shade of my aura.
when the trees are left bare,
i feel abandoned just like its many branches.

the sun finally shines through after several long months and i
remember what it feels like to be happy again.

~ light therapy

is mercury in retrograde right now?

because i also feel myself moving in the opposite direction of earth.

everything is going wrong- i can't express how i truly feel, i said something i didn't mean to someone i shouldn't have and my mind hasn't been thinking straight. i don't want to focus on anything much, i like my life is falling apart but no need to repair... i just need a few more weeks...

things will all be okay as soon as the planets realign.

~ liquid silver

close your eyes
and let the stars on your lids
take you to a galaxy far,
far away where you can always wake up from terrors,
and dreams always come true.

~ slumber

i experienced a lot of loss before any gain,
never knew love, just only felt pain...
so, when you tell me
that you adore every part of my being
how do you expect me
to even know what that means?

let me work on myself,
before i give my love to you.
allow me to guarantee that my energy will be pure,
and let me heal myself from wounds that happened
long before i met you,
so that you never have to
deal with them.

every morning,
i get out of bed
and thank the sun for shining in my window.

every night,
i lay back on the same pillows
and ask the moon to tell me the story on how it got its craters.

grateful to be here, yet curious of what lies beyond...
i dream of ways to someday be one with the sky
but for now, i'll settle with adoring its beauty from afar.

i find myself daydreaming often of an alternate universe
that i've created...

it's a parallel dimension
that only exists in the tranquility of my own mind.

it is a fantasy that i find myself living in,
a world that i seek to float off to in times of desolation
and i am at peace detaching myself from reality.

when i am there,
little can worry me,
i am free.

~ reverie

my heart was freshly broken,
nowhere near the healing stage.
i cried myself to sleep,
and woke up with puffy eyes.
i reached out to you hopeless,
wrote you a letter...
spilling all of my emotions.
i didn't care if you saw me venerable,
or thought that i was weak.
i told you my plans for us,
on how i could make things work.
it has been years and i still haven't heard back.
i was hurting inside,
drowning in an ocean of sorrow and misery,
but as time has gone on,
there were times where i wondered...
if your silence is what healed me.

woke up this morning,
smelling like the sage
i burned last night.
my mind was clear,
my spirit felt cleansed,
and i felt serenity
in carrying the scent with me all day long.

~ intentions

Chapter Four

FALLEN PETALS

a rose bush.

wild, untamed.

growing freely with thorns in every direction,

sprouting towards the sun.

branches dancing in the breeze...

suddenly red petals dwindle onto the ground, unattached from

everything they have ever known.

alone, each petal blows away in the wind,

descending into a world unseen.

blackened sun,

where is the light?

trying to find a ray of you with no luck.

blackened sun,

just like my soul,

dark and cold.

blackened sun,

why won't you rise?

~ stygian

a plucked flower possesses no beauty in the eyes of most.
to me, i see resilience.
the one feature that defines itself has been stripped away, yet the
flower still sustains its name.

you can take away my identity,
but you'll never change who i am.

tears as salty as the sea,
at times, i feel i am drowning in the ocean of your love.

~ rocky shores

my eyes used to have a certain purity to them.
i had an innocence in my intentions
and that all got stripped away,
unknowingly
the day i met you.

~ naive

the strings of love that tie us together are the same ones that
suffocate me.
i can't breathe in deep because my chest tightens as you wrap
your arms around me for a hug and it's impossible to part my
lips to inhale when you're kissing me.
i value loving you more than i do air.
you're all i want to breathe, no matter how much it hurts.

~ asphyxiated affection

i haven't felt like myself lately.
my favorite things
don't excite me anymore
and life lacks color.
my days are black and white.
i'm desperate to see a single shade of gray
to prove to me
that there is hope.

your lips were soft like a rose petal and you smelled just like one too... but making my way to caress your stem, a thorn pricked my finger and i bled.

~ scarlet red

i'm sure now
you realize
you were wrong
in so many ways.
i'm sure now
you realize
how much i'm worth...
and i'm sure now you realize
it's too late
to repair the damage.

you'll never know what it's like to be me,
to feel my pain.
you'll never know what it's like to lose yourself,
and not recognize who you've become or who you once were.
you'll never know what it's like to be me,
because i never did.

you give him an inch,
and he takes a mile.
you give him a smirk,
he asks for a smile.
he takes and he takes
until there's nothing left to give.

~ empty inside

i was strong today- at least that's what everyone tells me and i'm starting to believe it... because as my world was crumbling around me, i put the pieces together to form a smile.
that's strength.

i walked with my head held high and not a single tear visible in my eye. i can't cry or let them see me break because they think that i was strong today.

"i was strong today" i keep telling myself out loud, and figure the more times i say it, the more it will become true.

"i was strong today" i say once more as my voice begins to crack. i don't believe the words coming out my own mouth and i break down.

my strength is inadequate.

here now,
but in a flash,
gone without a trace...

you came and went
out my life so quickly,
almost as if you've done it before.

~ illusionist

i remember the feeling of happiness...
it was small things that kept me smiling.
i remember what it was like to feel joy,
my heart was full and my soul was shining.
i remember what it was like to feel comfort,
not ever thinking that my spirit could be broken.

sometimes i close my eyes,
and just remember.

suffering in silence
often seems like a better option
than letting others know of your pain.
they will use it as a weapon
and you will fall to your knees,
at the mercy of their ammunition
each and every time.

no one wanted
to hear her story
so she remained quiet
and allowed all the anger
to build up inside
until she just exploded
and no one knew why.
maybe they would have,
if they had only listened.

loneliness crawls over my skin,
and the pain begins to sink in.
tears fall from my face and
soaks the pillow i am laying on.
who knew i would feel so empty
without you here.

i realize i've just been
coasting through my life
with no real destination.
i cruise through my days…
hours feel like minutes,
months feel like days and
years continue to fly by.
when i look back
i see nothing
but a past of
unremarkable memories.

i spoke to you
and never once did you listen.
i cried to you
and you never wiped
a single tear from my eyes.
i reached out for help
and you didn't extend
your arms to pull me in close.

foolish of me to expect comfort
from the same source as my pain.

sanity seems so far away,
when only months ago it was within arm's reach.
i feel myself slipping away as the days go by,
and no longer recognize myself in the mirror.
i want my old self back.
the happy, cheerful me...
but then i wonder how on earth could
someone joyful be living inside this body?

even if it's deep inside...
even if i search and call out her name,
she's gotta be long gone by now.

your chest full of regret,
and your mind scripted with
the words that you think will mend my pain...

i don't need an apology.
your words never meant a thing before,
so why should i believe that they will hold weight now?

~ feathers

bright green leaves turn brown and slowly fall onto the base of an oak tree, losing its beauty... one by one, branches become exposed showing off its flimsy limbs and you think to yourself...

"how could something that stands so tall turn out to be so weak?"

i told you all of my deepest secrets,
ones that no one else knew.
i trusted you with every part of me
and never asked for a thing in return.
it broke my heart to see you leave,
and to this day
all i want back is the part of me
you took with you.

depression is when emptiness creeps in the cold night
and not even the brightest sunrise the next morning can
warm your soul.

~ horizon

my emotions show clear on my face and
no matter how much i try to disguise it,
you can see my eyes beginning to water,
and my face is as red as a burning flame.
my hands are clenched in a fist and
there's a knot building in my throat.
i'm hurting so much,
from holding it in so long
and at this point, i realize...
i couldn't hide my pain
even if i wanted to.

~ reveal

she loved you,
she cared for you,
she abandoned all she had for you...
gave up everything she owned,
to show you that you were her most prized possession,
and yet all you wanted to do was take ownership of the last
thing she had left...

which was herself.

~ cynical

imagine floating on your back
in the middle of the ocean,
with not a single other being in sight...
the sun reflecting off the waves and
being completely at peace...
then suddenly sinking into the abyss.
no one around to hear your cries and
not being strong enough
to pull yourself back to the surface.

say hello to my anxiety.

i'm sensitive, soft,
and thin-skinned.
criticism doesn't
sit well with me
and compliments
turn my face red.
i'd feel better
if i was invisible
so people couldn't
make comments at all.

i used to love you,
no matter how much you hurt me,
no matter how many times you made me cry.

i used to love you
no matter what my friends said,
i protected your actions and defended every accusation.

i used to love you,
no matter how much it pained me,
i continued to be by your side.

i used to love you,
even when i didn't feel it in return,
i loved every single part of you.

i used to love you.
i also used to love myself.

every touch feels electric.

every kiss, ecstatic... yet through time... your love - it burns.

~ lightning

black smoke clouds my mind as i think of you. it seeps from my head into my lungs... i breathe in your toxicity and it tastes acidic. no matter how many times i rinse out my mouth, i can't clean it enough.

i can't help but wonder how sweet life would have tasted without you.

~ bitter

coping with pain is difficult.
in many ways you wonder,
if others can rip my petals apart,
why can't i do the same?

i'll never know
how you moved on
and gave your heart to someone new.

i'll never know
how you learned to sleep
without me by your side,
because i never did.
i stay up every night
and weep at memories of what used to be.

i'll never know
how you managed to carry on after it all,
because i never did.
my heart aches every minute,
every hour,
every day.

i'll never know
how you moved on
and never felt any pain.

one of the main keys to happiness is finding beauty in destruction.

you destroyed me years ago and i have yet to find the beauty in that.

they always told me to watch out for fiery red ones like you but i
never felt your heat and your aura was my favorite color.
you disguised yourself so well and allowed me to mistake your
possessiveness for passion.

what i thought was a burning desire for my love turned out to be
the flame that burned us out.

~ blue devil

they tell you to write what your heart speaks but tell me...
what does an empty voice sound like?

~ heartbreak silence

the white doves
tell the black crow
that her wings are too broad
so she clips them.
they tell her that her feathers
are rough,
so she delicately smooths each one,
spending hours
to make sure they are perfect.
she is convinced
her beak is too long
as they mock her daily.

it is only when
the crow sees
the doves soar in the sky
with broad wings,
ruffled feathers and
extended beaks
does she realize
she no longer has the dexterity to fly,
quills to protect herself from the heat
or a beak for food to nourish her body—
does she caw
and wail in pain
at the changes she has made.

i knew you were no good for me
but i craved you anyways.

like a cigarette burning on my lips,
i tried giving you up many times...

but you continued to return,
and i always let you back in.

~ vice

running away from your problems never really solves anything, but what's the harm in wanting an escape? wanting it all to stop... begging the universe for a pause button.

it's one thing feeling lonely, and truly being alone – but feeling lonely in a room full of people is a stifling feeling.

it's like being at a concert and you're the only one who can't hear the music or not feeling the sunshine beaming on you when it's 87 degrees outside. you want to hear the music and feel the warmth, but you can't - so you run.

you run away and ignore every problem that comes ever so slightly in your direction... just hoping one day, you'd start feeling different... but you never do. you never feel anything really and then you just break – snap right in half... and we all know when something is broken, it's often not worth putting back together.

~ permanently damaged

the first time i ever experienced heartbreak,
was a day i'll never forget.
it was summer and the sun was shining.

it was also the first time the sun didn't actually feel as warm or
bright as it appeared, and i felt betrayed.

your lips like butter,
kissing you sends my heart numb.
i can't feel the pain you've caused anymore.
your lips melt away the hurt
as you glide your fingers through my hair.

~ soft

prison. trapped. caged.

mentally lost in a maze.

which way is out, which way was in?

where is the end and the beginning?

reality seems further than it was before.

i see the light leading the way out of this darkness only to find out it is the light from the sun that burns my soul and skin instead of nourishing the brightness that was once within.

lost. confused. dazed.

mentally broken with no cure. my soul is fractured and my heart is sore.

the ending for me is near.

i gave all of myself to you.
i loved you for how you made me feel...
now that you're gone, i don't feel a thing
and forgot how to love myself.

you drained me of my worth
and i'm left with nothing.

~ empty

don't you understand?
how you stripped me from my sanity...
how i stayed up late at night,
wishing you would call...

sometimes i would stay up so late
that i would hear your voice
lingering in the back of my ear
but you were never there.

i invited you in.

you didn't have to knock at the door, or even ring the bell.

i welcomed you so openly to the comfort of my heart just for you to burn down all four walls.

after the smoke clears and black soot fades away... there's nothing left but a dead bolt on the door.

don't bother knocking or ringing the bell...

no one is home.

do not cry when i am gone, for weeping will not breathe life back into my body and do not lay flowers by my grave, for they will simply die as well.

my emotions manifest themselves into violence. my shaking hand turns into a balled-up fist and my breathing is heavy enough to be heard across the room.

i'm angry because i love you. the way you say my name makes me want to pull my hair and when you hold me, my nails dig deep into your skin. i hate that i'm in love with you. i hate your unconditional acceptance of who i am and who i once was. i hate when you tell me everything is going to be okay when it won't be and most of all, i hate that you love me more than i love myself.

don't accept, assure or adorn me.

i am not worthy of your love and it makes me angry, so i push you away only hoping that one day you'll get fed up... so fed up that you'll leave and find someone deserving of your affection but for now my balled-up fist and heavy breathing only make you want to calm me down and this only makes me hate to love you even more.

during the day,
i dread the feeling of falling asleep...
knowing that you are all i will dream about.

at night, i pray that there comes a day...
where i wake up,
and you don't cross my mind.

i do not fear what is to come.
i fear what has already happened.

how can i allow new memories to enter,
when the troubled thoughts of my past
have invaded my mind
and are here to stay?

how can i dream of tomorrow
when i'm lost in the despair of yesterday?

i cannot rid my history of its demons and i think that is what i fear
the most.

the silence in this room is deafening.
you're by my side but,
i've never felt so alone.
the words can't seem to come out,
yet i have so much to say...
so, we just sit
in silence.

~ hush

i miss the days being surrounded by your warmth so much that i didn't even need the sun and the nights where your eyes twinkled more than my favorite star in the sky.

the voices in my head
sound just like fairies in a garden
whispering, giggling, and laughing the afternoon away.
i want to join them
and ask how their skin glimmers in the sunlight but
i've been told not to pay them any mind
so i take my daily dose,
and slowly but surely
the voices go away…
but not to worry,
it'll only be until tomorrow
when the fairies come back out to play.

you love me, you love me not.
plucking away my petals and tossing them onto the ground as you
tell me how much i mean to you.
ripping off all the pieces of me, stripping my being completely,
as each petal descends into the dirt.

i believe you, i believe you not.
unsure of how i truly feel, all i can muster up to say amidst all the
pain is "i love you too".

sometimes love just isn't enough.

~ oxeye daisy

my heart aches most first thing in the morning.
after a long night of letting my mind rest and
forgetting that you're no longer a part of me...

i wake up to the realization of what is,
and it breaks me.

after a seemingly endless winter, where my surroundings have been so harsh... i no longer feel imprisoned.

being able to lay here with my back on the ground, reaching my arms freely towards the sun - i am able to close my eyes and feel the warmth.

no longer am i subjected to deal with the bleak and cold world. i am here – basking in the summer's light for eternity.

happiness at last.

~ felo de se

kisses from her lips as lustrous as silk,
skin smooth like velvet.
her body was elegant like chiffon,
yet her heart was as thick as wool.

~ fabrication

Chapter Five

FULLY BLOOMED

my soul is a flower that flourishes in the sunlight of struggle.
it is watered by the waves of my tears and packed down with the
soil of my pain. this flower has been planted many times and
ripped out just as much. its leaves have withered up and fallen... its
petals have been plucked and the stem has been cut from its ripped
roots. withered and worn, dried out and dying... fallen and
forgotten...

this flower is my soul that flourishes in the sunlight of struggle and
there's plenty of sunlight around.

sun rays beam around me and the heat warms up my soul
like the first day i met you.

a small gust of wind wraps around me the same way your
arms once did and i feel free.

the grass on my toes connects me to mother nature's
existence as i lay there and think of you.

~ love is what summer feels like

i've always been protective
over my heart and emotions,
guarding them
like a warden over his prisoners,
but loving you has released that shield
and i've opened my mind to the fact
that loving you may be the best thing i've ever done.

~ lock and key

tell me what you want.
teach me how to love you.
show me what makes you happy,
so i can do it right.
i've never had the chance...
to be with someone quite like you.
i need to learn this thing called love
one step at a time.

like a soft ballad that
puts you in a trance,
i can't help but sing along
to the rhythm of your heartbeat
because it's my favorite song.

when the sun goes down
and the stars come out to play
is when i come alive.
the moonlight twinkles in my eyes
and shines right in my window
brighter than the most powerful
rays of sunshine.
i do not fear the darkness
because that is what is inside of me.

~ night owl

the hardest part of loving you
was learning you,
but i enjoyed every lesson...
and it's only now that i know,
that what is worth having,
won't come easy.

~ discovery

your love flows through me like the blood in my veins, your touch it heals me, internally, it takes away my pain.

the sound of your voice soothes me and your heartbeat, it's the soundtrack to my soul.

when you look into my eyes, it's like you see who i am, you think i'm more precious than gold.

being in your presence takes me somewhere new, and i'll tell you - it's honestly breathtaking to be standing here on earth, when your world is standing in front of you.

to gaze at your beauty
is to stare into the eyes of perfection.
i could do this all day long
and would never grow weary.

coming from a lack of self-love,
to an abundance of admiration...
was an overwhelming journey
but it is not simply my reflection in the mirror
that brings me so much joy...
it is the reflection of my past—
realizing where i am now
and how far i've come...
that makes me love who i am
more than ever before.

you possess everything i lack.
you are patient when i am unwilling,
you are loving when i am angry,
you are warmth and light,
when i am nothing but the cold darkness.

~ yang

ocean waves crash onto the sand and as the cold water rushes to my toes, i smell salt in the air.

i've wanted to drown in these very waters before but being safe at shore feels just fine to me.

i used to despise the light
and find comfort in the darkness.
i surrounded myself in the shadows
and hid from sunrays beaming in my window.
i kept all the lights off inside
and summer was my least favorite time of year...
but one day i finally let the warmth
and glow from outside find its way in
and i haven't been the same ever since.

~ vampire diaries

the thunder outside rumbles,
and lightning strikes in the distance.
rain begins to fall against my windowpane
and i find tranquility in the storm.

some days
i want to be left alone
other times i crave the presence
of anyone besides my own
because the solitary
becomes lonesome.

it's only for awhile
after company joins,
that i push them away in hopes
of pure isolation.

~ moody

you sent me falling
without a parachute
but you were there to catch me
before my feet even touched the ground.

if i could go back in time,
i wouldn't change a single thing.
i would knowingly make all of the same mistakes...
love openly, cry often,
and allow myself to feel the same pain as before.
these experiences mapped out the story of my life,
so i feel blessed to have had them...
and i wouldn't alter my recovery,
even if i could.

the finest paintbrush couldn't portray your one sided shallow dimple and the thickest one wouldn't be able to stroke your beautiful locks of hair on canvas.

what a masterpiece you are.
you are my muse and biggest inspiration.

~ one of a kind

a thousand petals have fallen,
completely bare...
nothing left but sepal.
a thousand petals have fallen,
yet i still stand tall.
a thousand petals have fallen,
yet i am grateful...
to have had them fallen at all.

it took quite some time for me to feel this way but
i'm in love with you.
every morning that i wake up and get to see your face is a blessing.
to know that i once wanted nothing but to rid this world of your
existence pains me but i am now painfully in love with you.
you are me, i am you.

you are my reflection and i will love you until the end of time.

i'm tired of blaming you
for all my all my anger and angst.
i no longer want to hold you accountable
for me feeling this way.
when i am asked what is the reason for my pain,
i do not want your name to cross my mind.
when i am crying late at night and wondering why,
i don't want scenes of you breaking
my spirit replaying in my head.
when i am told by others that everything will be alright,
i want to believe it.
i've realized all of my desires
are up to me to fulfill.
so today i am taking control of it all...
because i'm tired of blaming you
for all my anger and angst.

do you think about me?
when you reflect on all those you love, do i make it on the list?

do you dream about me?
when you drift off to sleep after a long day, am i the image you see
when you close your eyes?

do you speak about me?
when people ask who i am, do your eyes light up as you say my
name?

do you love me?
when your heart skips a beat is it because of me?

think about me. dream about me. speak about me. love me.

endlessly. effortlessly. eternally.

when i'm with you,
i feel strong.
every weak thought
that crosses my mind
evaporates into the air
and disappears from existence.

when i'm with you, i feel invincible.

to be in love is to sacrifice
to sacrifice is to take away
to take away is to strip one's self
to strip yourself is to be left with nothing
to be left with nothing is emptiness
to be empty is to seek fulfillment.
to seek fulfillment is to seek love.
to seek love is to fall in love
to fall in love is to be in love
to be in love is to sacrifice

~ annulus

if i could go back to the day,
to when i first met you...
i'd let the universe replay our initial encounter
where butterflies filled my stomach,
and my heart smiled inside my chest.

i would do anything
to experience your love
for the very first time all over again.

i'm changing my ways
of fearing the unknown.
i'm taking control of my life
and i've never been more excited,
because another day isn't promised.
there will be no more what ifs or maybes...
i'm existing in the now.

so, if tomorrow never comes,
just know that i lived today.

my love for you runs deep like the ocean.

my heart, bottomless with emotion.

my love for you is gentle, like the sound of rain and
although it can come down hard and fast, it is worth
waiting for the sun to shine afterwards.

every day i wake up and look into the mirror. my nappy hair covers my big forehead and my bulging eyes look back at me in the reflection.

every day i wake up, worrying what challenges i will face as a black woman, what mountains i will have to trek and what oceans i may drown in.

every day i wake up feeling like i have the world on my shoulders, so heavy that i can barely hold my head high.

every day i wake up and admire myself in the mirror. my curly coils bounce free and my chocolate brown eyes can see the world crystal clear.

every day i wake up, anticipating what great things this black woman can do, what mountains i can climb and what deep waters i can swim through.

every day i wake up strong enough to have the world on my shoulders while walking miles with my crown held high... ***because*** i am a black woman.

something within me feels like i've been here before,
like i've lived this life and loved you already.
when i close my eyes, images of our future flash in my mind and
when i open them, i see you here with me. this journey together
was planned out long before we crossed paths. long before you said
hello and long before i thought i fell in love with you.
i was made for you.

born to be loved by you.

i never wanted to burden you
with my woes and worries
but you were always there with a listening ear
which made it easy to continue my tirades.
i cried on your shoulder
more nights than i can count.
i'm grateful for many of your attributes
but most thankful that you wiped my tears
and showed me how to smile again.

in a world so large,
it's easy to feel small...
and with so many roads to travel,
it's easy to get lost...
but i find comfort in being held in your arms
and always feeling at home.

you are the crisp breath of air i breathe first thing in the morning. you are the breakfast that nourishes my body and gives me the strength to make it through the day. you're the moonlight that shines in my window when i fall asleep at night. you are my sunrise, my sunset and everything in between.

you are my strength. when i am weak, you lift me up. my spirit, soul and body are risen because of you. i am indebted to you, my forever love.

those tears you cry
are proof that you are still here
so, dry your eyes
and rejoice in the light of the sun,
for today is a new day,
and anything is possible.

Acknowledgments

first acknowledgement goes to you... yes, you. a writer is nothing without a reader. thank you for being intrigued enough to hear what i had to say.

thank you to my mom... for supporting and loving me through this journey. not just the journey of creating this book, but the entire journey of my life, actually. you've constantly encouraged me to do whatever my heart desires. not everyone in life is so lucky.

thank you to the few people that are close to me who knew i was writing this book and always cheered me on. you know who you are.

strangely enough, i also want to thank anyone who has ever hurt or challenged me. many of the emotions i've evoked in this book wouldn't have been possible without those folks. my personal growth wouldn't have been possible without them, either. i found love in their hate and discovered peace within pain.

Postface

when i started working on this book, i became distant. i was focused... but distant... disconnected from a lot in my life. it took nearly four years to complete. i went through so many things during that time. good and bad. there were times where i was hurting, and writing healed me. there were other times where i felt like i had nothing to write about and had to dig into the pain of my past in order to complete this project. that was tough. there were times where i had joyful moments in stages of my life and i'm happy to have documented them in the form of poetry.

there were times where i didn't know if i was ever going to finish... or if i even wanted to finish. i questioned allowing any and everyone to see inside my head... but i just kept going. i kept writing and spilling my thoughts. before i knew it, i was a few pages away from being done and realized this was one of my biggest accomplishments. i told myself that even if it only gets read by 12 people and they all hate it... i'm so glad to have done it. the experience was my therapy.

i would have never thought that something good would ever come from what i've been through, but i'm so proud of these pages.

i don't have anything profound to say... i just want to thank you for taking the time to read my words.

eternally grateful.

if you enjoyed this book, please leave a review online. feel free to keep up with me via my website below, as well as to find out about any upcoming projects.

fullybloomed.net

Printed in Great Britain
by Amazon

43324202R00116